Quick Vegetarian
Main Dishes

Whether you consider yourself a full-time vegetarian
or someone who's looking to try something
different, the recipes in this collection are sure
to please! We've collected some of our favorite
vegetarian main dish recipes from recent cookbooks
and featured them in this collection. From salads
to soups to pastas and more, you'll find easy and
quick recipes to prepare for any occasion.

Enjoy!

The Pampered Chef® Test Kitchens

On the front cover: *Harvest Brown Rice Salad*, p. 25.

On the back cover: *Sweet Potato Tagine with
Pine Nut Couscous*, p. 57.

artichoke & red bell pepper risotto

OUR VERSION OF THIS CREAMY ITALIAN RICE DISH FEATURES
A PLEASING COMBINATION OF TENDER VEGETABLES.

Total Time: 28 minutes   **Yield:** 6 servings

5-6 cups (1.25-1.5 L) vegetable broth, divided

2 jars (7.5 oz or 170 mL each) quartered marinated artichoke hearts, drained, divided

3 shallots

1 tbsp (15 mL) olive oil

1½ cups (375 mL) uncooked Arborio rice

1½ cups (375 mL) dry white wine such as Chardonnay

1 lemon

1 small red bell pepper

½ cup (125 mL) frozen peas

2 oz (60 g) cream cheese, softened

2 oz (60 g) Parmesan cheese, grated (about ½ cup/125 mL)

Snipped fresh chives (optional)

1 Heat broth in **(2-qt./1.9-L) Saucepan** over medium-high heat until simmering. Reduce heat to medium-low. Meanwhile, place artichokes into **Executive (12-in./30-cm) Skillet** (do not use stainless cookware); sauté over medium-high heat 4-5 minutes or until light golden brown. Remove from Skillet; reserve ½ cup (125 mL) of the artichokes. Set aside remaining artichokes.

2 Meanwhile, finely chop shallots using **Santoku Knife**. Add oil, shallots and rice to Skillet; cook and stir 1-2 minutes or until shallots are tender and rice is shiny and translucent. Add wine; cook 1-2 minutes or until wine is completely evaporated, stirring with **Small Bamboo Spatula**. Carefully add 1 cup (250 mL) of the broth to Skillet; cover and cook 2-3 minutes or until liquid is absorbed, stirring occasionally. Repeat with remaining broth in 1-cup (250-mL) increments, cooking 2-3 minutes after each addition or until liquid is absorbed (13-15 minutes total cook time, see Cook's Tip). Remove Skillet from heat.

3 Meanwhile, zest lemon with **Microplane® Adjustable Grater** to measure 1 tbsp (15 mL). Cut bell pepper into 1-in. (2.5-cm) pieces. Stir remaining artichokes, zest, bell pepper, peas, cream cheese and Parmesan cheese into rice. Top with reserved artichokes and garnish with snipped fresh chives, if desired.

U.S. Nutrients per serving: Calories 380, Total Fat 11 g, Saturated Fat 3.5 g, Cholesterol 15 mg, Carbohydrate 52 g, Protein 11 g, Sodium 780 mg, Fiber 5 g

U.S. Diabetic exchanges per serving: 3½ starch, 2 fat (3½ carb)

COOK'S TIPS

Risotto is typically cooked by adding the broth in increments. When rice is completely cooked, it should have a creamy texture with a slight bite in the center of the rice grain. Adding the liquid slowly allows the rice to slowly cook and release the starches. This prevents the rice from becoming gummy.

Shallots lend a combination of both onion and garlic flavors and add a hidden depth because when finely chopped, they virtually melt into the food.

caprese pizzas

REFRIGERATED PIZZA DOUGH GIVES YOU A HEAD START ON THIS ITALIAN CLASSIC. THE DOUGH IS CUT INTO THREE LONG STRIPS FOR A DRAMATIC PRESENTATION.

Total Time: 29 minutes   **Yield:** 6 servings

Toppings

- 3 medium tomatoes
- 1 tsp (5 mL) salt
- 2 tbsp (30 mL) chopped fresh basil leaves
- 1 tbsp (15 mL) **Basil Oil** or olive oil
- 8 oz (250 g) fresh mozzarella cheese
- Coarsely ground black pepper

Crusts

- 1 tsp (5 mL) plus 1 tbsp (15 mL) Basil Oil or olive oil, divided
- 1 pkg (13.8 oz or 283 g) refrigerated pizza crust
- 1 garlic clove, pressed
- 1 oz (30 g) Parmesan cheese, grated (about ¼ cup/50 mL)

1 Preheat oven to 425°F (220°C). For toppings, slice tomatoes into ¼-in. (6-mm) slices. Place onto paper towel-lined **Cutting Board**. Sprinkle both sides evenly with salt; let stand 15 minutes.

2 Meanwhile, for crusts, using **Chef's Silicone Basting Brush**, lightly brush **Rectangle Stone** with 1 tsp (5 mL) of the oil. Unroll dough onto baking stone. Press garlic into **(1-cup/250-mL) Prep Bowl** and combine with remaining 1 tbsp (15 mL) oil; brush over dough. Grate Parmesan cheese using **Rotary Grater**; sprinkle evenly over dough. Cut dough lengthwise into thirds with **Pizza Cutter**. Carefully move dough strips slightly apart on baking stone. Bake 11-12 minutes or until bottoms of crusts are light golden brown.

3 Meanwhile, chop basil using **Santoku Knife** (see Cook's Tip); combine with oil in another Prep Bowl and set aside for later use. Blot tops of tomato slices with paper towels. Slice mozzarella cheese into ¼-inch-thick (6-mm) slices. Arrange tomato and cheese slices in overlapping rows on baked crusts. Return to oven; bake an additional 4-5 minutes or until cheese melts.

4 Remove baking stone from oven to **Stackable Cooling Rack**. To serve, brush basil mixture over pizzas and sprinkle with black pepper.

U.S. Nutrients per serving: Calories 350, Total Fat 18 g, Saturated Fat 7 g, Cholesterol 35 mg, Carbohydrate 34 g, Protein 14 g, Sodium 960 mg, Fiber 2 g

U.S. Diabetic exchanges per serving: 2 starch, 1 vegetable, 1 medium-fat meat, 2 fat (2 carb)

COOK'S TIPS

Salting tomatoes pulls out the excess moisture, preventing a soggy pizza. Blotting well with paper towels results in a more concentrated flavor.

To easily chop basil, stack leaves on top of each other and roll into a tight cylinder. Slice crosswise to form ribbons. Turn basil ribbons and slice crosswise again.

zesty ravioli skillet

IT'S AMAZING THAT SUCH A FRESH AND FLAVORFUL DISH STARTS WITH FROZEN RAVIOLI AND ONLY TAKES ABOUT 20 MINUTES TO PREPARE.

Total Time: 20 minutes   **Yield:** 8 servings

- 4 cups (1 L) loosely packed fresh baby spinach leaves
- 6 oz (175 g) provolone cheese, grated
- 1 tbsp (15 mL) olive oil
- 1 small jalapeño pepper, seeded
- 3 garlic cloves, pressed
- 2 cans (14.5 oz or 398 mL each) diced tomatoes with onions, undrained
- ½ tsp (2 mL) salt
- ½ tsp (2 mL) coarsely ground black pepper
- 1 pkg (24 oz/700 g) small frozen cheese ravioli (about 65)
- ⅓ cup (75 mL) heavy whipping cream

1 Wash spinach in large **Stainless Mesh Colander**; drain. Grate cheese using **Ultimate Mandoline** fitted with grating blade. Set aside spinach and cheese.

2 Add oil to **(12-in./30-cm) Skillet**; heat over medium-high heat 1-3 minutes or until shimmering. Finely chop jalapeño with **Food Chopper**. Add jalapeño to Skillet; cook and stir 1 minute or until crisp-tender. Press garlic into Skillet with **Garlic Press**; cook and stir 15-20 seconds or until fragrant.

3 Add tomatoes, salt and black pepper to Skillet; cook and stir with **Bamboo Spatula** 1-2 minutes or until simmering. Add ravioli; stir to coat. Cook, uncovered, 4-5 minutes or until tender. Stir cream into Skillet. Cook, uncovered, 1-2 minutes or until simmering. Sprinkle spinach over ravioli; cook, covered, 1 minute or until spinach starts to wilt.

4 Remove Skillet from heat. Top with cheese; cover Skillet and let stand 1-2 minutes or until cheese is melted.

U.S. Nutrients per serving: Calories 330, Total Fat 14 g, Saturated Fat 7 g, Cholesterol 50 mg, Carbohydrate 38 g, Protein 13 g, Sodium 650 mg, Fiber 3 g

U.S. Diabetic exchanges per serving: 2 starch, 1 vegetable, 1 high-fat meat, 1 fat (2 carb)

COOK'S TIPS

Half and half can be substituted for the heavy whipping cream, if desired.

Wear plastic gloves when working with jalapeño peppers. The juice from the peppers can create a burning sensation on the skin.

For a dish with more heat, do not seed the jalapeño pepper.

If desired, a 24-oz (700-g) package of large cheese-filled ravioli can be substituted for the small ravioli. Add ½ cup (125 mL) water to Skillet with tomatoes. Increase ravioli cook time to 8 minutes in Step 3.

green vegetable minestrone

SERVE THIS AUTHENTIC ITALIAN SOUP WITH A SIDE OF CRISPY FLATBREAD.

Total Time: 20 minutes   **Yield:** 6 servings

1 tsp (5 mL) olive oil

1 medium onion

5 garlic cloves, pressed

8 cups (2 L) vegetable broth

1 cup (250 mL) uncooked ditalini pasta

½ tsp (2 mL) salt

½ tsp (2 mL) coarsely ground black pepper

8 oz (250 g) green beans, trimmed

1 medium zucchini

1 can (15 oz or 540 mL) cannellini beans, drained and rinsed

1½ oz (45 g) Parmesan cheese, grated (about 6 tbsp/90 mL)

¼ cup (50 mL) snipped fresh parsley

¼ cup (50 mL) prepared pesto

1 Add oil to **(4-qt./3.8-L) Casserole**; heat over medium-high heat 1-3 minutes or until shimmering. Meanwhile, chop onion with **Santoku Knife**. Add onion and garlic pressed with **Garlic Press** to Casserole; cook 1-3 minutes or until onion is tender.

2 Add broth, pasta, salt and black pepper to Casserole; bring to a boil. Meanwhile, cut green beans and zucchini into ½-in. (1-cm) pieces. Reduce heat to medium; add vegetables and cannellini beans. Cook 8-10 minutes or until pasta is tender. Grate cheese using **Rotary Grater** and snip parsley using **Professional Shears**. Ladle soup into serving bowls. Top with pesto, cheese and parsley.

U.S. Nutrients per serving (1³/₄ cups/425 mL): Calories 250, Total Fat 7 g, Saturated Fat 2 g, Cholesterol 5 mg, Carbohydrate 37 g, Protein 10 g, Sodium 1250 mg, Fiber 6 g

U.S. Diabetic exchanges per serving: 2 starch, 1 vegetable, 1½ fat (2 carb)

COOK'S TIPS

Ditalini pasta is a small, tube-shaped pasta. Other small pasta shapes such as orzo can be substituted.

Pesto is made from basil, garlic, pine nuts, Parmesan cheese and olive oil. Prepared pesto is an easy way to add fresh flavor to dishes. It can be found in the produce section of most major grocery stores.

For a quick homemade pesto, finely chop 1 cup (250 mL) loosely packed fresh basil leaves and ¼ cup (50 mL) toasted pine nuts or walnuts; place into a medium bowl. Add 1 oz (30 g) finely grated fresh Parmesan cheese, ¼ cup (50 mL) olive oil and 2 pressed garlic cloves; mix well.

ricotta gnocchi with brown butter sauce

MADE WITH TWO TYPES OF CHEESE IN THE PLACE OF MASHED POTATOES, THESE TENDER PAN-FRIED MORSELS WILL DISAPPEAR AS FAST AS YOU CAN MAKE THEM.

Total Time: 23 minutes   **Yield:** 4 servings

- 1 lemon, divided

- 1 cup (250 mL) whole milk ricotta cheese

- 2 oz (60 g) Parmesan cheese, grated (about ½ cup/125 mL)

- 1 egg

- ½ tsp (2 mL) salt

- ½ cup (125 mL) all-purpose flour, plus additional for dusting

- ¼ cup (50 mL) butter (½ stick), divided

- 2 tbsp (30 mL) olive oil

- ½ tsp (2 mL) crushed red pepper flakes

- 1 garlic clove, pressed

- 1 tbsp (15 mL) snipped fresh parsley

- Fresh baby spinach leaves and shaved Parmesan cheese (optional)

1 Zest lemon using **Microplane® Adjustable Grater** to measure 1 tsp (5 mL). Set lemon aside for use in sauce. Combine zest, cheeses, egg and salt in **Classic Batter Bowl**; mix well. Fold in flour just until incorporated (do not overmix). Lightly flour a 13-in. (33-cm) piece of **Parchment Paper**. Using **Small Scoop**, drop 28 level scoops of ricotta mixture onto Parchment Paper, forming gnocchi.

2 Add 1 tbsp (15 mL) of the butter and oil to **Executive (12-in./30-cm) Skillet** (do not use stainless cookware); heat over medium-high heat 4-5 minutes or just until butter mixture begins to brown. Add gnocchi to Skillet. Cook 2-3 minutes on each side or until golden brown, turning with **Sauté Tongs**. Remove gnocchi from Skillet and keep warm.

3 Reduce heat to medium. Add remaining 3 tbsp (45 mL) butter to Skillet; cook 3-5 minutes or until butter is a deep brown color, occasionally swirling Skillet. Juice lemon to measure 1 tsp (5 mL). Remove Skillet from heat. Immediately add juice, pepper flakes, pressed garlic and parsley, swirling to combine. Serve gnocchi with sauce. If desired, serve with fresh baby spinach leaves and shaved Parmesan cheese.

U.S. Nutrients per serving: Calories 400, Total Fat 31 g, Saturated Fat 16 g, Cholesterol 125 mg, Carbohydrate 15 g, Protein 15 g, Sodium 670 mg, Fiber 1 g

U.S. Diabetic exchanges per serving: 1 starch, 2 high-fat meat, 3 fat (1 carb)

COOK'S TIPS

There is no need to shape these gnocchi. The Small Scoop does most of the work for you. As the gnocchi are cooked, they flatten and resemble scallops.

If desired, part-skim milk ricotta can be substituted for the whole milk ricotta.

spicy roasted vegetable soup

Total Time: 29 minutes   **Yield:** 6 servings

1 medium red bell pepper

1 medium onion

1 can (14.5 oz or 398 mL) petite diced tomatoes, undrained

1 cup (250 mL) loosely packed fresh cilantro

2 garlic cloves, peeled

1 chipotle pepper in adobo sauce

½ tsp (2 mL) salt

1 large red potato, unpeeled (about 1 cup/ 250 mL diced)

2 medium zucchini or yellow squash (about 3 cups/750 mL diced)

4 cups (1 L) vegetable broth

1 can (15 oz or 398 mL) black beans, drained and rinsed

Lime wedges, warm tortillas and sour cream (optional)

1 Preheat broiler. Chop bell pepper and onion into 2-in. (5-cm) pieces. Place onto **Medium Sheet Pan**; spray vegetables with vegetable oil using **Kitchen Spritzer**. Place pan 2-4 in. (5-10 cm) from heating element. Broil 5-7 minutes or until lightly charred and softened. Place roasted vegetables, tomatoes, cilantro, garlic, chipotle pepper and salt into blender container. Cover and blend until smooth.

2 Meanwhile, dice potato and zucchini into ½-in. (1-cm) cubes. Place potato and broth into **(4-qt./3.8-L) Casserole**. Bring to a simmer over medium heat; cook 6-8 minutes or until potato begins to soften. Add roasted vegetable mixture to Casserole. Cook 7-8 minutes or until potato is tender, skimming often with **Skimmer**. Add zucchini and beans. Cook 4-5 minutes or until zucchini is tender. Serve with lime wedges, tortillas and sour cream, if desired.

U.S. Nutrients per serving (about 1⅓ cups/325 mL): Calories 90, Total Fat 1 g, Saturated Fat 0 g, Cholesterol 0 mg, Carbohydrate 20 g, Protein 4 g, Sodium 930 mg, Fiber 5 g

U.S. Diabetic exchanges per serving: ½ starch, 2 vegetable (½ carb)

COOK'S TIPS

For best flavor, use an all-natural vegetable broth that does not contain mushrooms.

Leftover chipotle peppers can be stored in the freezer. Arrange chipotle peppers in a single layer in a resealable plastic freezer bag. When a recipe calls for chipotle peppers, simply break off the number of peppers you need.

spanish-style stuffed peppers

STEAMING THESE PEPPERS IN THE MICROWAVE MAKES
THIS RECIPE EVEN FASTER TO PREPARE.

Total Time: 29 minutes **Yield:** 4 servings

- 1 pkg (5 oz or 175 g) yellow saffron rice (plus ingredients to make rice)
- 2 medium red bell peppers
- 2 medium tomatoes
- 1 poblano pepper or small green bell pepper
- 1 green onion with top
- ¼ cup (50 mL) chopped fresh cilantro, divided
- 1 tsp (5 mL) olive oil
- 2 garlic cloves, pressed
- ¾ cup (175 mL) shredded Mexican cheese blend, divided
- 2 tbsp (30 mL) water

1 Prepare rice according to package directions in **(1.5-qt./1.4-L) Saucepan**. As rice cooks, prepare bell peppers. Slice bell peppers in half lengthwise; remove and discard stems and seeds. Microwave, covered, in **Large Micro-Cooker®** on HIGH 3-4 minutes or until crisp-tender. Carefully remove bell peppers and pat dry with paper towels.

2 Meanwhile, core and seed tomatoes with **Core & More**. Using **Santoku Knife**, dice tomatoes and poblano pepper. Slice green onion. Chop cilantro.

3 Add oil to **(10-in./24-cm) Skillet**; heat over medium heat 1-3 minutes or until shimmering. Add tomatoes, poblano pepper, onion, half of the cilantro and garlic pressed with **Garlic Press**; cook 2-3 minutes or until onion is tender.

4 Stir vegetable mixture and ½ cup (125 mL) of the cheese into rice in Saucepan. Place bell peppers cut side up into Skillet; spoon rice mixture evenly into each pepper and sprinkle with remaining cheese. Add water to Skillet. Cover Skillet and heat over medium-low heat 3-5 minutes or until cheese is melted. Sprinkle with remaining cilantro.

U.S. Nutrients per serving (½ pepper): Calories 250, Total Fat 8 g, Saturated Fat 4.5 g, Cholesterol 20 mg, Carbohydrate 35 g, Protein 9 g, Sodium 620 mg, Fiber 2 g

U.S. Diabetic exchanges per serving: 2 starch, ½ vegetable, ½ medium-fat meat, 1 fat (2 carb)

COOK'S TIP

We used packaged yellow saffron rice, available in most grocery stores, to save time in preparing this recipe. Yellow rice is flavored with onion and garlic as well as saffron, the most expensive spice in the world. Saffron adds a unique flavor and a beautiful color to the rice.

tomato-basil soup with ricotta dumplings

THE TENDER AND DELICATE DUMPLINGS STAND OUT IN THIS SIMPLE SOUP.

Total Time: 30 minutes **Yield:** 2 servings

Soup

- 1 tsp (5 mL) **Basil Oil** or olive oil
- 1 garlic clove, pressed
- 1 can (15 oz or 398 mL) crushed tomatoes, undrained
- 1½ cups (375 mL) vegetable broth
- ¼ cup (50 mL) snipped fresh basil leaves

Dumplings

- ¼ cup (50 mL) part-skim ricotta cheese
- 2 tbsp (30 mL) grated fresh Parmesan cheese
- 1 egg white, lightly beaten
- ½ tsp (2 mL) salt
- ¼ tsp (1 mL) coarsely ground black pepper
- ⅓ cup (75 mL) all-purpose flour

  Thinly sliced fresh basil leaves

1 For soup, combine oil and garlic in **(3-qt./2.8-L) Saucepan**; cook and stir over medium heat 1-2 minutes or just until garlic begins to turn light golden brown. Immediately add tomatoes, broth and basil. Bring to a boil. Reduce heat; simmer 5-7 minutes, stirring occasionally.

2 Meanwhile, for dumplings, combine ricotta cheese, Parmesan cheese, egg white, salt and black pepper in **Small Batter Bowl**; mix well. Add flour; stir just until combined. Using **Small Scoop**, scoop dumpling mixture directly into simmering soup. Cook until dumplings float to the surface, about 2 minutes. Remove from heat. Ladle soup into bowls; sprinkle with thinly sliced fresh basil.

U.S. Nutrients per serving (about 1½ cups/375 mL): Calories 250, Total Fat 7 g, Saturated Fat 2.5 g, Cholesterol 15 mg, Carbohydrate 36 g, Protein 13 g, Sodium 1400 mg, Fiber 6 g

U.S. Diabetic exchanges per serving: 2 starch, 1 vegetable, 1 medium-fat meat (2 carb)

COOK'S TIPS

Soup should be gently simmering when dumplings are added. Do not boil soup or the tender dumplings may break apart. Serve soup soon after cooking dumplings to maintain their texture.

For the most tender dumplings, carefully measure flour by lightly spooning into cup and leveling off with a knife. Do not overmix the batter once the flour has been added.

poached eggs florentine

THE UNIQUE CROUTONS GIVE THIS CLASSIC EGG DISH AN ELEGANT PRESENTATION.

Total Time: 28 minutes   **Yield:** 4 servings

Croutons

4 slices firm white sandwich bread

Vegetable oil

Spinach Mixture

1 pkg (10 oz/300 g) frozen chopped spinach

¾ cup (175 mL) heavy whipping cream

½ cup (125 mL) shredded Swiss cheese

2 garlic cloves, pressed

½ tsp (2 mL) salt

Poached Eggs

8 cups (2 L) water

2 tbsp (30 mL) white vinegar

8 eggs

Salt (optional)

Paprika (optional)

1 Preheat oven to 350°F (180°C). For croutons, slice crusts off bread with **Bread Knife**; discard crusts. Cut bread into ¼-in. (6-mm) strips; arrange in a single layer on **Medium Round Stone with Handles** and lightly spray with oil using **Kitchen Spritzer**. Bake 15-20 minutes or until golden brown. Remove from oven.

2 Meanwhile, microwave spinach according to package directions using **Small Micro-Cooker®**. Line large **Colander** with several paper towels; add spinach. Fold over towels and squeeze out water; remove spinach from towels and place into **(1.5-qt./1.4-L) Saucepan**. Add cream, cheese, garlic pressed with **Garlic Press** and salt; cook and stir over medium heat 4-6 minutes or until cheese is melted.

3 For eggs, bring water and vinegar to a boil in **(12-in./30-cm) Skillet**; reduce heat to a gentle simmer. Crack one egg into **(1-cup/250-mL) Prep Bowl** and gently add to water; repeat with remaining eggs (see Cook's Tip). Carefully move **Skimmer** under eggs to prevent sticking; cook 3-5 minutes or according to desired doneness. Remove eggs with Skimmer to paper towel-lined plate; season with salt, if desired.

4 To serve, spoon creamed spinach evenly onto serving plates; arrange croutons around edges. Top each serving with two eggs and sprinkle with paprika, if desired.

U.S. Nutrients per serving (2 eggs): Calories 430, Total Fat 32 g, Saturated Fat 16 g, Cholesterol 495 mg, Carbohydrate 17 g, Protein 21 g, Sodium 700 mg, Fiber 2 g

U.S. Diabetic exchanges per serving: 1 starch, ½ vegetable, 2½ medium-fat meat, 3½ fat (1 carb)

COOK'S TIPS

To poach eggs to even doneness, slide the first egg into the water closest to the handle (this will provide a marker for your starting point). Add the remaining eggs clockwise around the edge of the Skillet. When eggs are cooked, remove with the Skimmer in the same order for best results.

Vinegar is added to the poaching water to help the eggs keep their shape and to keep the egg whites from spreading out or becoming stringy. If desired, lemon juice can be substituted for the vinegar.

For croutons with added flavor, spray bread with **Garlic Oil** using Kitchen Spritzer before toasting.

persian chickpea salad

THIS SALAD HAS A PLEASINGLY SPICY DRESSING OFFSET WITH COOL MINT.
RINSING THE CHOPPED ONION REMOVES SOME OF THE "BITE."

Total Time: 20 minutes **Yield:** 4 servings

Dressing

1 lemon

1 tbsp (15 mL) olive oil

½ tsp (2 mL) cinnamon

½ tsp (2 mL) ground cumin

½ tsp (2 mL) salt

¼ tsp (1 mL) ground cayenne pepper

Salad

1 can (19 oz or 540 mL) chickpeas

½ small red onion

1 4-in. (10-cm) piece seedless cucumber

3 medium plum tomatoes

2 tbsp (30 mL) thinly sliced fresh mint leaves

2 oz (60 g) queso fresco or feta cheese

Toasted pita bread (optional, see Cook's Tip)

1 For dressing, juice lemon to measure 3 tbsp (45 mL). Whisk together lemon juice, oil, cinnamon, cumin, salt and cayenne pepper in **Classic Batter Bowl**.

2 For salad, drain and rinse chickpeas in small **Colander**. Chop onion using **Santoku Knife** and place into **(7-in./18-cm) Strainer**; rinse under cold running water. Drain onion and pat dry with paper towel.

3 Chop cucumber; seed and chop tomatoes. Add chickpeas, onion, cucumber and tomatoes to dressing; toss to coat. Thinly slice mint and fold into salad.

4 Dice queso fresco. Serve each salad topped with queso fresco and toasted pita bread, if desired.

U.S. Nutrients per serving: Calories 130, Total Fat 6 g, Saturated Fat 1 g, Cholesterol 5 mg, Carbohydrate 16 g, Protein 6 g, Sodium 490 mg, Fiber 4 g

U.S. Diabetic exchanges per serving: ½ starch, 2 vegetable, 1 fat (½ carb)

COOK'S TIPS

Rinsing onion under running water takes away the sharpness of raw onion. This technique is also great to use when preparing homemade salsa.

Queso fresco is a mild, fresh Mexican cheese and is similar to Persian fresh cheese called panir.

For toasted pita bread, preheat oven to 450°F (230°C). Split 5 miniature whole-wheat pita bread rounds (about 3 in./7.5 cm) in half horizontally, then vertically with **Color Coated Tomato Knife**. Arrange pita bread in a single layer on **Large Round Stone with Handles**; bake 5-6 minutes or until lightly toasted. Remove from oven.

chilled summer soup with black bean relish

THIS DELICIOUS, EYE-CATCHING SOUP OFFERS A GARDEN'S BOUNTY OF VEGETABLES AND DOESN'T REQUIRE ANY COOKING AT ALL.

Total Time: 14 minutes **Yield:** 4 servings

Soup

- 2 medium cucumbers
- 4 green onions with tops
- 1½ cups (375 mL) vegetable broth
- 1 cup (250 mL) frozen peas
- 2 garlic cloves, peeled
- 3 limes
- 1 avocado, peeled and pitted
- ¼ tsp (1 mL) salt
- ⅛ tsp (0.5 mL) coarsely ground black pepper

Relish and Garnish

- 1 small red bell pepper
- 2 green onions with tops
- 1 can (15 oz or 540 mL) black beans, drained and rinsed
- 1 garlic clove, pressed
- Reserved lime juice from soup
- ¼ tsp (1 mL) salt
- ⅛ tsp (0.5 mL) coarsely ground black pepper
- ¼ cup (50 mL) sour cream
- *Chipotle Tortilla Chips* (optional, see Cook's Tip)

1 Peel cucumbers using **Serrated Peeler**. Slice cucumbers crosswise into thirds using **Santoku Knife**; remove seeds using **The Corer™**. Slice green onions into thirds. Add cucumbers, onions, broth, peas and garlic to blender container; cover and blend until smooth. Juice limes to measure 5 tbsp (75 mL); reserve 2 tbsp (30 mL) for relish. Add avocado, remaining 3 tbsp (45 mL) juice, salt and black pepper to blender; cover and blend until smooth.

2 Cut bell pepper into ½-in. (1-cm) pieces and thinly slice onions. Toss together bell pepper, onions, beans, pressed garlic, reserved juice, salt and black pepper in **Small Batter Bowl**. Ladle soup into serving bowls; top with relish and sour cream. Serve with chips, if desired.

U.S. Nutrients per serving (1½ cups/375 mL): Calories 210, Total Fat 10 g, Saturated Fat 3 g, Cholesterol 10 mg, Carbohydrate 26 g, Protein 7 g, Sodium 790 mg, Fiber 10 g

U.S. Diabetic exchanges per serving: 1½ starch, 1 vegetable, 1½ fat (1½ carb)

COOK'S TIPS

The Corer™ makes quick work of removing the seeds from a cucumber. Peel the cucumber and slice it crosswise into thirds to make the tool work most efficiently.

The acid in the lime juice helps maintain this soup's bright green color. This recipe can be stored, covered, in the refrigerator for up to one day. Stir well before serving.

For *Chipotle Tortilla Chips*, preheat oven to 400°F (200°C). Brush one side of 4 (6-in./15-cm) flour tortillas with 1 tsp (5 mL) olive oil; sprinkle with ¼ tsp (1 mL) **Chipotle Rub**. Cut each tortilla into eight wedges; arrange in a single layer on **Rectangle Stone**. Bake 12-14 minutes or until edges are light brown.

harvest brown rice salad

THE SLIGHTLY BITTER FLAVOR OF RADICCHIO IS BALANCED BY THE SWEETNESS
OF OUR SWEET CINNAMON SPRINKLE IN THIS COLORFUL SALAD.

Total Time: 25 minutes **Yield:** 4 servings

2 tbsp (30 mL) olive oil, divided

2 cups (500 mL) uncooked instant brown rice

1½ cups (375 mL) apple cider

½ tsp (2 mL) salt

⅓ cup (75 mL) sweetened dried cranberries

1 tbsp (15 mL) butter, melted

1 medium red baking apple such as Jonathan

2 tbsp (30 mL) **Sweet Cinnamon Sprinkle**

1 large head radicchio

5 stalks celery

3 tbsp (45 mL) chopped fresh chives

½ cup (125 mL) toasted walnuts or *Cinnamon-
Glazed Walnuts* (see Cook's Tip)

2 oz (60 g) crumbled goat cheese

1 For rice mixture, add 1 tbsp (15 mL) of the oil to **(1.5-qt./1.4-L) Saucepan**; heat over medium heat 1-3 minutes or until shimmering. Add rice; stir until well coated with oil. Stir in cider and salt. Bring to a boil. Cover; reduce heat to low. Simmer 5 minutes; remove from heat. Stir in cranberries; cover and let stand 5 minutes.

2 Meanwhile, for apple, heat **Grill Pan** over medium-high heat 5 minutes. Place butter into **(1-cup/250-mL) Prep Bowl**; microwave on HIGH 30-60 seconds or until melted. Core apple using **The Corer™**; slice crosswise into ¼-in. (6-mm) rings. Brush both sides of apple rings with butter; sprinkle with cinnamon sprinkle, gently pressing to adhere to apple.

3 Spray Grill Pan with vegetable oil using **Kitchen Spritzer**. Grill apple rings 1 minute on each side or until grill marks appear. Remove from pan. Set aside six apple rings for garnish. Cut remaining apple rings into quarters; add to rice mixture.

4 Add rice mixture to **Stainless (4-qt./4-L) Mixing Bowl**; cool slightly. Set aside four large outer leaves of radicchio for later use. Thinly slice remaining radicchio using **Chef's Knife**. Thinly slice celery on a bias; chop chives. Toss vegetables and remaining 1 tbsp (15 mL) oil with rice mixture. To serve, spoon salad into reserved radicchio leaves; garnish with walnuts and reserved apple rings. Sprinkle with crumbled goat cheese.

U.S. Nutrients per serving: Calories 600, Total Fat 25 g, Saturated Fat 7 g, Cholesterol 20 mg, Carbohydrate 85 g, Protein 11 g, Sodium 460 mg, Fiber 7 g

U.S. Diabetic exchanges per serving: 4 starch, 1 fruit, 1 vegetable, 4 fat (5 carb)

COOK'S TIPS

Cinnamon-Glazed Walnuts: Combine 2 tbsp (30 mL) Sweet Cinnamon Sprinkle, 1 tbsp (15 mL) butter, 1 tbsp (15 mL) corn syrup and ⅛ tsp (0.5 mL) salt in **(8-in./20-cm) Sauté Pan**. Stir over medium heat until butter is melted. Add 1 cup (250 mL) walnuts and cook, stirring constantly, 5-7 minutes or until walnuts are fragrant. Spread walnuts in a single layer on **Parchment Paper**. Cool completely.

If you do not have Sweet Cinnamon Sprinkle, lightly sprinkle apple rings with sugar after brushing with butter.

portobello, red pepper & goat cheese pizza

THE CRUST OF THIS ROBUST, MEATLESS PIZZA IS GRILLED ON BOTH SIDES, DOUBLING THE GREAT GRILLED FLAVOR.

Total Time: 30 minutes   **Yield:** 4 servings

Vinaigrette

- ¼ cup (50 mL) **Garlic Oil** or olive oil
- 2 tbsp (30 mL) red wine vinegar
- 2 garlic cloves, pressed
- 1 tsp (5 mL) finely chopped fresh thyme leaves
- ½ tsp (2 mL) salt
- ¼ tsp (1 mL) coarsely ground black pepper

Pizza

- 12 oz (350 g) portobello mushrooms (about 6 medium)
- 1 medium red bell pepper
- 1 10-oz (300-g) prebaked thin pizza crust
- 1 pkg (4 oz/125 g) crumbled goat cheese, divided

1 Prepare grill for direct cooking over medium-high heat. For vinaigrette, whisk together ingredients in **Small Batter Bowl**. Reserve 2 tbsp (30 mL) in **(1-cup/250-mL) Prep Bowl** for serving.

2 For pizza, remove stems from mushrooms with **Paring Knife**. Cut bell pepper in half; remove stem and seeds. Brush both sides of pizza crust with vinaigrette. Grill vegetables, covered, 8-9 minutes or until tender, turning and brushing occasionally with vinaigrette using **BBQ Basting Brush**. Remove vegetables from grill using **BBQ Tongs**.

3 Place pizza crust top side down onto grid of grill. Grill, covered, 1-2 minutes or until slighly browned and crisp. Turn crust over with **BBQ Turner**; top with goat cheese, reserving 1 tbsp (15 mL) for garnish. Grill an additional 1-2 minutes or until bottom of crust is browned and crisp. (Cheese will soften but not appear melted.) Remove crust from grill.

4 Slice bell pepper into thin strips and mushrooms on a bias using **Santoku Knife**. Arrange mushrooms and bell pepper over crust. Drizzle reserved vinaigrette evenly over top. Sprinkle with reserved goat cheese, if desired.

U.S. Nutrients per serving: Calories 450, Total Fat 27 g, Saturated Fat 8 g, Cholesterol 30 mg, Carbohydrate 38 g, Protein 17 g, Sodium 810 mg, Fiber 3 g

U.S. Diabetic exchanges per serving: 2 starch, 1 vegetable, 1 high-fat meat, 4 fat (2 carb)

COOK'S TIPS

Watch the pizza crust closely. If the crust starts to brown unevenly, rotate it on the grill as necessary.

Look for prepared thin pizza crusts in the bread aisle of your grocery store.

Crumbled feta cheese can be substituted for the crumbled goat cheese, if desired.

If desired, ¼ tsp (1 mL) dried thyme can be substituted for the fresh thyme leaves in the dressing.

tofu parmigiana with fire-roasted tomatoes

EXTRACTING EXTRA MOISTURE FROM EXTRA-FIRM TOFU CREATES
A UNIQUE BASE FOR AN ITALIAN CLASSIC.

Total Time: 20 minutes   **Yield:** 4 servings

1 pkg (14 oz or 350 g) extra-firm tofu, drained

¾ tsp (4 mL) salt, divided

½ tsp (2 mL) coarsely ground black pepper, divided

1 small onion

1 can (14.5 oz or 398 mL) diced fire-roasted tomatoes

2 garlic cloves, pressed

½ oz (15 g) Parmesan cheese, grated (about 2 tbsp/30 mL packed)

½ cup (125 mL) panko bread crumbs

1 tsp (5 mL) **Italian Seasoning Mix**

1 egg

2 tbsp (30 mL) olive oil, divided

¼ cup (50 mL) shredded part-skim mozzarella cheese

¼ cup (50 mL) loosely packed fresh basil leaves

1. Pat tofu dry with paper towels, removing as much moisture as possible. Slice tofu horizontally into eight ½-inch-thick (1-cm) slices. Season tofu with ½ tsp (2 mL) of the salt and ¼ tsp (1 mL) of the black pepper.

2. Finely chop onion with **Food Chopper**. Combine onion, tomatoes, pressed garlic, remaining ¼ tsp (1 mL) salt and ¼ tsp (1 mL) black pepper in **Small Micro-Cooker®**. Microwave on HIGH 6 minutes or until heated through. Meanwhile, grate Parmesan cheese with **Microplane® Adjustable Grater**. Combine Parmesan cheese, bread crumbs and seasoning mix in first **Coating Tray**. Lightly beat egg in second tray. Dip each tofu slice into egg and then into bread crumb mixture, coating generously.

3. Add 1 tbsp (15 mL) of the oil to **(12-in./30-cm) Skillet**; heat over medium heat 1-3 minutes or until shimmering. Add four tofu slices to Skillet. Cook 1-2 minutes or until golden brown. Turn tofu over; sprinkle with half of the mozzarella cheese and cook 1-2 minutes or until coating is golden brown. Remove from Skillet; repeat with remaining oil, tofu and mozzarella cheese. Thinly slice basil. Serve tofu with sauce and basil.

U.S. Nutrients per serving: Calories 270, Total Fat 16 g, Saturated Fat 3.5 g, Cholesterol 60 mg, Carbohydrate 15 g, Protein 17 g, Sodium 800 mg, Fiber 3 g

U.S. Diabetic exchanges per serving: 1 starch, 2 medium-fat meat, 1 fat (1 carb)

COOK'S TIPS

Patting the tofu dry with paper towels removes excess moisture, which helps to achieve a crisp crust. Make sure to purchase extra-firm tofu for this recipe to keep the slices intact during coating and cooking.

Italian-seasoned diced tomatoes can be substituted for the fire-roasted diced tomatoes, if desired.

corn & poblano chowder

RICHLY FLAVORED POBLANO PEPPERS ADD EXCITEMENT
TO THIS FRESH CORN CHOWDER.

Total Time: 27 minutes   **Yield:** 4 servings

- 4 ears corn, husks and silk removed
- 2 cups (500 mL) whole milk
- 2 cups (500 mL) vegetable broth
- 1 medium onion
- 2 poblano peppers
- 2 tbsp (30 mL) butter
- ¼ cup (50 mL) all-purpose flour
- ½ tsp (2 mL) salt
- ½ tsp (2 mL) coarsely ground black pepper
- 1 medium carrot, peeled

1. Remove corn kernels from cobs using **Kernel Cutter**; set aside. Break cobs in half. Place cobs, milk and broth in **Classic Batter Bowl** (see Cook's Tip); microwave on HIGH 8 minutes. Carefully remove batter bowl from microwave. Carefully remove and discard cobs from milk mixture using **Chef's Tongs**.

2. Meanwhile, chop onion and poblanos with **Chef's Knife**. Add butter to **(4-qt./3.8-L) Casserole**; melt over medium heat. Add onion, poblanos, corn kernels and flour; cook and stir 7-9 minutes or until onion is tender. Add milk mixture, salt and black pepper; bring to a boil. Cut carrot into julienne strips using **Julienne Peeler**. Ladle chowder into large mugs; top with carrot strips.

U.S. Nutrients per serving (1½ cups/375 mL): Calories 290, Total Fat 11 g, Saturated Fat 6 g, Cholesterol 25 mg, Carbohydrate 43 g, Protein 10 g, Sodium 880 mg, Fiber 5 g

U.S. Diabetic exchanges per serving: 2 starch, 1 high-fat milk (3 carb)

COOK'S TIPS

It pays to invest the extra time needed to prepare fresh corn in this recipe. The corn cobs release starch into the milk mixture as they are heated, helping to thicken the chowder.

Perhaps best known for chiles rellenos, peppers stuffed with cheese, poblano peppers are dark green Mexican peppers with a full-bodied flavor. They can range from mild to rather spicy. Green bell peppers can be substituted for poblano peppers, if desired.

moroccan ravioli

HUMMUS PROVIDES THE BASE FOR THE UNIQUE FILLING IN THESE RAVIOLI.

Total Time: 29 minutes **Yield:** 4 servings

Sauce

- ½ lemon
- ¼ tsp (1 mL) salt
- 1 tbsp (15 mL) olive oil
- 2 garlic cloves, pressed
- 1 tbsp (15 mL) **Moroccan Rub**
- ⅓ cup (75 mL) vegetable broth
- ½ tsp (2 mL) sugar
- ⅓ cup (75 mL) heavy whipping cream

Ravioli

- ¾ cup (175 mL) shredded reduced-fat mozzarella cheese
- ½ cup (125 mL) roasted red pepper hummus
- 1 tbsp (15 mL) Moroccan Rub
- 8 (7-in./18-cm) egg roll wrappers
- 1 egg white, lightly beaten
- 1 tbsp (15 mL) olive oil, divided
- ⅔ cup (150 mL) water, divided

1 Slice lemon half into ¼-in. (6-mm) slices using **Chef's Knife**. Sprinkle lemon slices with salt and place in **(1-cup/250-mL) Prep Bowl**. Microwave on HIGH 1 minute or until slices are softened. Heat oil, pressed garlic and rub in **(1.5-qt./1.4-L) Saucepan** over medium-high heat 2-3 minutes or until fragrant. Add broth and sugar. Bring to a boil; boil 3-5 minutes. Add cream; cook 1-2 minutes or until mixture thickens slightly. Finely chop lemon slices. Remove Saucepan from heat; stir in lemon.

2 In **Small Batter Bowl**, combine cheese, hummus and rub; mix well. Brush four wrappers with egg white. Using **Small Scoop**, place level scoop of hummus mixture onto each corner of the wrappers, leaving a 1-in. (2.5-cm) border around edges. Place remaining wrappers over filling; press around filling to seal. Cut each wrapper into four squares with **Pastry Cutter** fitted with fluted wheel.

3 Add ½ tbsp (7 mL) of the oil to **(12-in./30-cm) Skillet**; heat over medium heat 1-3 minutes or until shimmering. Place half of the ravioli in Skillet; cook 1-2 minutes or until bottoms are golden brown. Add ⅓ cup (75 mL) of the water to Skillet; cover immediately. Cook ravioli 1-2 minutes or until water is evaporated and ravioli are tender. Remove ravioli. Wipe out Skillet; add remaining ½ tbsp (7 mL) oil. Repeat with remaining ravioli and water. Serve ravioli with sauce.

U.S. Nutrients per serving: Calories 440, Total Fat 22 g, Saturated Fat 8 g, Cholesterol 45 mg, Carbohydrate 46 g, Protein 14 g, Sodium 1190 mg, Fiber 3 g

U.S. Diabetic exchanges per serving: 3 starch, 1 medium-fat meat, 3 fat (3 carb)

COOK'S TIPS

Plain or garlic-flavored hummus can be substituted for the roasted red pepper hummus, if desired.

Preserved lemons are common in Moroccan cooking and take weeks to prepare conventionally. Our quick method of "preserving" lemons is done in less than 5 minutes.

crunchy breakfast tacos

HERE IS AN INTERESTING TWIST ON BREAKFAST THAT THE WHOLE FAMILY
WILL ENJOY. A QUICK BLENDER SALSA IS ADDED TO
EGGS AFTER THEY ARE SOFT-SET.

Total Time: 25 minutes **Yield:** 4 servings

Tomatillo Salsa

8 oz (250 g) tomatillos (about 3 medium tomatillos), husks removed

1 jalapeño pepper, stemmed

1/4 cup (50 mL) loosely packed fresh cilantro

1/2 tsp (2 mL) salt

Tacos

1/4 cup (50 mL) chopped fresh cilantro

1 medium tomato

8 hard yellow corn taco shells

1 cup (250 mL) shredded Mexican cheese blend, divided

6 eggs

2 tbsp (30 mL) water

1 tbsp (15 mL) butter

1 Preheat oven to 350°F (180°C). For salsa, bring water to a boil in **(2-qt./1.9-L) Saucepan**. Add tomatillos and jalapeño; cook 5-8 minutes or until tomatillos are tender. Meanwhile, for tacos, chop cilantro and dice tomato using **Santoku Knife**; set aside.

2 To finish salsa, transfer tomatillos from Saucepan to blender container using **Slotted Spoon**. Remove jalapeño from Saucepan; test for spiciness (see Cook's Tip). Add desired amount of jalapeño to blender; cover and blend until smooth. Add cilantro and salt; blend 2 seconds or until cilantro is coarsely chopped.

3 To finish tacos, line up taco shells, side by side, in **Medium Bar Pan**; fill with half of the cheese. Bake 5-6 minutes or until cheese is melted. Remove from oven.

4 As taco shells bake, whisk eggs and water in **Small Batter Bowl**. Place butter in **Executive (10-in./24-cm) Skillet** (do not use stainless cookware); heat over medium heat 1-3 minutes or until foamy. Add eggs; cook and stir 2-3 minutes or until eggs begin to set. Add 1/4 cup (50 mL) of the salsa; cook 1-2 minutes or until eggs are completely set. To serve, spoon eggs evenly into shells; sprinkle with remaining cheese, cilantro and tomato. Serve with remaining salsa.

U.S. Nutrients per serving (2 tacos): Calories 370, Total Fat 25 g, Saturated Fat 11 g, Cholesterol 350 mg, Carbohydrate 19 g, Protein 18 g, Sodium 710 mg, Fiber 2 g

U.S. Diabetic exchanges per serving: 1 starch, 1 vegetable, 2 medium-fat meat, 2 1/2 fat (1 carb)

COOK'S TIPS

Tomatillos are also referred to as "husk tomatoes" because of their papery outer skins. Tomatillos are quite tart and are typically cooked before using. When buying tomatillos, the husks should be fresh looking, not brown and wrinkled. The fruit should be firm to the touch and not "splitting" the husk.

The heat level of jalapeño peppers can vary widely. To test for spiciness, cut off and taste the end. It's best to add the jalapeño pepper conservatively; it's far easier to spice up a mild salsa than to try to reduce the heat once too much has been added.

To save even more time in the morning, substitute prepared salsa verde for the tomatillo salsa.

grilled portobello bruschetta

THIS AUTHENTIC ITALIAN DISH FEATURES GRILLED PORTOBELLO
MUSHROOMS PLACED ON GRILLED BREAD AND LAYERED WITH
SMOKED MOZZARELLA AND FRESH ARUGULA.

Total Time: 22 minutes **Yield:** 4 servings

- 4 slices (3/4-in./2-cm thick) Vienna or Italian bread
- 2 tbsp (30 mL) **Garlic Oil**
- 4 large portobello mushroom caps (4-5 in./10-13 cm in diameter each)
- 1/2 cup (125 mL) light balsamic vinaigrette salad dressing, divided
- 1 cup (250 mL) cherry tomatoes
- 6 oz (175 g) smoked mozzarella cheese (see Cook's Tip)
- 4 cups (1 L) fresh arugula
- 1 oz (30 g) Asiago cheese

1 For bread, heat **Grill Pan** over medium heat 5 minutes. As pan heats, slice bread on a slight bias using **Bread Knife**. Brush both sides of bread with oil. Place bread into pan. Grill bread 1 minute on each side or until grill marks appear. Remove from pan and set aside.

2 As bread grills, start toppings. Brush mushrooms with 2 tbsp (30 mL) of the vinaigrette. Place mushrooms into pan. Grill 4-5 minutes on each side or until grill marks appear and mushrooms are tender. Remove from pan to **Cutting Board**.

3 As mushrooms grill, cut tomatoes into quarters; set aside. Slice mozzarella cheese into twelve 1/4-inch-thick (6-mm) slices.

4 To serve, place bread onto serving plates. Place three mozzarella cheese slices onto each bread slice. Slice mushrooms on a bias and arrange over cheese. Arrange tomatoes around bruschetta; drizzle tomatoes and mushrooms with 1/4 cup (50 mL) of the vinaigrette. Toss arugula with remaining vinaigrette and arrange over bruschetta. Using **Vegetable Peeler**, shave Asiago cheese over arugula. Serve immediately.

U.S. Nutrients per serving: Calories 390, Total Fat 23 g, Saturated Fat 8 g, Cholesterol 30 mg, Carbohydrate 25 g, Protein 18 g, Sodium 1030 mg, Fiber 3 g

U.S. Diabetic exchanges per serving: 1 1/2 starch, 1 vegetable, 2 medium-fat meat, 2 fat (1 1/2 carb)

COOK'S TIPS

Smoked mozzarella cheese infuses any dish with a distinctive smoky flavor and is a great melting cheese. It can be found in the gourmet cheese section of larger grocery stores packaged in mini-loaves, slices or balls.

Arugula is an aromatic salad green with a peppery flavor. Watercress or baby spinach leaves can be substituted for the arugula, if desired.

lightning-fast veggie chili

THIS HEARTY CHILI IS JUMP-STARTED BY SIMMERING TOMATOES,
CHILI POWDER AND GARLIC IN THE LARGE MICRO-COOKER®.

Total Time: 28 minutes **Yield:** 4 servings

- 1 can (28 oz or 796 mL) diced tomatoes, undrained
- 3 garlic cloves, pressed
- 1 tbsp (15 mL) chili powder
- ½ tsp (2 mL) salt
- 1 medium yellow squash
- 1 medium onion
- 1 medium poblano pepper
- 1 tsp (5 mL) olive oil, divided
- 3 tbsp (45 mL) tomato paste
- 1 can (16 oz or 450 g) chili beans in sauce, undrained
- ¼ cup (50 mL) chopped fresh cilantro
- Shredded cheddar cheese and sour cream (optional)

1 Combine tomatoes, pressed garlic, chili powder and salt in **Large Micro-Cooker®**; microwave on HIGH 5-7 minutes or until simmering. Remove from microwave and set aside.

2 Meanwhile, seed and dice squash using **Petite Paring Knife**. Dice onion and poblano using **Santoku Knife**. Add ½ tsp (2 mL) of the oil to **(4-qt./3.8-L) Casserole**; heat over medium-high heat 1-3 minutes or until shimmering. Add squash; cook 1-2 minutes or until tender. Set squash aside.

3 Add remaining ½ tsp (2 mL) oil to Casserole; cook onion and poblano 3-4 minutes or until tender. Add tomato paste and cook 30 seconds or until tomato paste begins to caramelize, stirring constantly.

4 Add tomato mixture to Casserole. Reduce heat to medium-low; add beans and squash. Simmer 4-5 minutes or until chili is thickened, stirring occasionally.

5 As chili simmers, chop cilantro. Stir cilantro into chili; serve with cheese and sour cream, if desired.

U.S. Nutrients per serving: Calories 210, Total Fat 2 g, Saturated Fat 0 g, Cholesterol 0 mg, Carbohydrate 39 g, Protein 9 g, Sodium 1300 mg, Fiber 11 g

U.S. Diabetic exchanges per serving: 2 starch, 2 vegetable (2 carb)

COOK'S TIPS

The fresh vegetables are sautéed for the best flavor, then combined with tomato mixture, which is started in the microwave for a slow-cooked taste.

Tomato paste lends depth to this dish. Allowing it to slightly caramelize enhances the flavor of the chili.

For an interesting twist, serve over multi-grain tortilla chips with shredded cheese, or use as a great topping for baked potatoes.

stovetop cheese enchiladas

NO ONE WILL BELIEVE THAT THESE DELICIOUS ENCHILADAS
WERE MADE ON THE STOVETOP IN JUST 30 MINUTES!

Total Time: 30 minutes **Yield:** 12 servings

Enchilada Sauce

- 6 pasilla chiles, stemmed and seeded
- 4 cups (1 L) water
- ½ large onion
- 1 medium plum tomato
- 1 can (14.5 oz) vegetable broth (about 1¾ cups/425 mL)
- 1 garlic clove, peeled
- 1 tsp (5 mL) salt
- 1 tsp (5 mL) sugar

Enchiladas

- 24 (6-in./15-cm) corn tortillas
- ½ large onion
- 1½ lbs (750 g) grated Chihuahua or Monterey Jack cheese, divided (about 8 cups/2 L)

1. For sauce, place chiles and water into **Large Micro-Cooker®**. Microwave, covered, on HIGH 6-8 minutes or until chiles are softened; drain. Coarsely chop onion using **Santoku Knife**. Add sauce ingredients to blender container; cover and blend until smooth. Press sauce through (**7-in./18-cm**) **Strainer** into (**2-qt./1.9-L**) **Saucepan** using **Classic Scraper**. (Discard fibrous strings.) Bring sauce to a boil. Reduce heat to low; cook 3-5 minutes or until heated through.

2. Meanwhile, for enchiladas, place tortillas in dry Large Micro-Cooker®; microwave, covered, on HIGH 2 minutes or until softened. Chop onion. Reserve 1 cup (250 mL) of the cheese for later use. Add onion and remaining cheese to **Stainless (4-qt./4-L) Mixing Bowl**; mix well.

3. Place about 2 tbsp (30 mL) of the cheese mixture onto each tortilla. Roll up tortillas and place seam side down on **Double Burner Griddle**. Pour sauce evenly over enchiladas. Top with reserved cheese. Tent with foil; cook over medium heat 5-7 minutes or until cheese is completely melted and enchiladas are heated through.

U.S. Nutrients per serving (2 enchiladas): Calories 330, Total Fat 18 g, Saturated Fat 11 g, Cholesterol 60 mg, Carbohydrate 29 g, Protein 15 g, Sodium 670 mg, Fiber 2 g

U.S. Diabetic exchanges per serving: 2 starch, 1 medium-fat meat, 2 fat (2 carb)

COOK'S TIPS

Pasilla chiles are dried chiles that are about 6-8 in. (15-20 cm) long and are blackish-brown in color. They can be found in the ethnic section of most grocery stores.

This recipe can be made on the **Large Bar Pan**. Preheat oven to 450°F (230°C). Assemble enchiladas as directed and place onto pan; tent with foil sprayed with nonstick cooking spray. Bake 10 minutes or until cheese is melted.

If you don't have time to make your own enchilada sauce, substitute with 3½ cups (875 mL) of your favorite store-bought sauce.

creamy one-pot pasta

THIS ONE-POT WONDER COMBINES SLIVERED GARLIC AND FRESH VEGETABLES FOR A LIGHT PASTA DISH YOUR FAMILY WILL BE SURE TO REQUEST AGAIN.

Total Time: 20 minutes   **Yield:** 6 servings

4 garlic cloves, peeled

1 jar (7 oz or 210 mL) sun-dried tomatoes in oil, undrained

3 cans (14.5 oz each) vegetable broth (5¼ cups/1.25 L)

1 lb (450 g) uncooked penne pasta

1 head broccoli (2 cups/500 mL small florets)

2 medium carrots, peeled

4 oz (125 g) reduced-fat cream cheese (Neufchâtel)

½ tsp (2 mL) coarsely ground black pepper

¼ tsp (1 mL) salt

Grated fresh Parmesan cheese and snipped fresh basil leaves (optional)

1   Slice garlic using **Garlic Slicer**. Place garlic and 1 tbsp (15 mL) oil from sun-dried tomatoes into **(8-qt./7.6-L) Stockpot**; cook over medium heat 2-3 minutes or until garlic is golden brown, stirring occasionally. Remove from heat; add broth. Return Stockpot to burner; increase heat to high. Cover and bring to a boil. Add pasta; cover and simmer vigorously 8-10 minutes or until pasta is almost cooked but still firm, stirring occasionally using **Mega Scraper**.

2   Meanwhile, cut broccoli into small florets; place into **Classic Batter Bowl**. Cut carrots in half lengthwise; thinly slice crosswise on a bias. Drain tomatoes; pat dry and slice into thin strips.

3   Cut cream cheese into cubes. Add vegetables, cream cheese, black pepper and salt to pasta; stir until cream cheese is melted and fully incorporated. Reduce heat to medium; cover and cook an additional 2-4 minutes or until vegetables are tender. If desired, top with Parmesan cheese and basil.

U.S. Nutrients per serving: Calories 410, Total Fat 10 g, Saturated Fat 3.5 g, Cholesterol 15 mg, Carbohydrate 66 g, Protein 15 g, Sodium 1090 mg, Fiber 5 g

U.S. Diabetic exchanges per serving: 3½ starch, 2 vegetable, 2 fat (3½ carb)

COOK'S TIPS

For an interesting flavor twist, omit black pepper, salt, Parmesan cheese and basil. Add 1 tbsp (15 mL) **Moroccan Rub** or **Greek Rub**.

Don't throw away remaining oil from the jar of sun-dried tomatoes. Reserve it to make salad dressing or pesto.

If desired, 2 cups (500 mL) halved cherry tomatoes can be substituted for the sun-dried tomatoes.

spicy broccoli frittata

THIS FRITTATA STARTS OUT ON THE STOVETOP AND IS FINISHED
IN THE OVEN TO KEEP IT TENDER AND MOIST THROUGHOUT.

Total Time: 29 minutes   **Yield:** 6 servings

4 oz (125 g) cream cheese, softened

8 eggs

2 tbsp (30 mL) water

1 tbsp (15 mL) Dijon mustard

1 head broccoli (2 cups/500 mL small florets)

2 green onions with tops

2 plum tomatoes

1 tbsp (15 mL) butter

½-1 tsp (2-5 mL) crushed red pepper flakes

1 cup (250 g) shredded mozzarella cheese, divided

1. Preheat oven to 350°F (180°C). Whisk cream cheese until smooth in **Classic Batter Bowl**; gradually add eggs, water and mustard and whisk until smooth. Cut broccoli into small florets using **Santoku Knife**. Slice onions into ½-in. (1-cm) pieces; thinly slice tomatoes.

2. Place butter and pepper flakes into **Executive (10-in./24-cm) Skillet** (do not use stainless cookware); heat over medium heat 1-2 minutes or just until pepper flakes begin to brown. Immediately add broccoli and onions; cook 1-2 minutes or until onions begin to soften. Pour egg mixture into Skillet; cook and stir 3-4 minutes or until eggs are almost set. Top evenly with half of the cheese and tomato slices; sprinkle with remaining cheese.

3. Bake 12-15 minutes or until center of egg mixture is set but still moist and internal temperature reaches 155°F (68°C). Carefully remove Skillet from oven using **Oven Mitts**; let stand 5 minutes (temperature will rise to 160°F/71°C). Serve immediately.

U.S. Nutrients per serving: Calories 240, Total Fat 18 g, Saturated Fat 9 g, Cholesterol 320 mg, Carbohydrate 5 g, Protein 15 g, Sodium 350 mg, Fiber 1 g

U.S. Diabetic exchanges per serving: 1 vegetable, 2 medium-fat meat, 1½ fat (0 carb)

COOK'S TIPS

Cooking the red pepper flakes for a few minutes activates the natural oils in the dried pepper and brings out the spiciness.

Frittatas are a versatile anytime meal because you can use a variety of vegetables and cheeses, as well as herbs and spices to create your own distinctive dish.

Asparagus can be substituted for the broccoli, if desired.

To quickly soften cream cheese, microwave on HIGH 15-20 seconds.

hot & sour soup

Total Time: 28 minutes **Yield:** 6 servings

- 6 cups (1.5 L) vegetable broth, divided
- 4 dried shiitake mushrooms
- 3 green onions with tops
- ¼ cup (50 mL) rice vinegar
- ¼ cup (50 mL) reduced-sodium soy sauce
- 1-2 tsp (5-10 mL) Thai red curry paste
- 2 medium carrots
- 3 tbsp (45 mL) cornstarch
- ¼ cup (50 mL) water
- 1 pkg (14 oz or 350 g) tofu (see Cook's Tip)
- 3 eggs

1 Pour ½ cup (125 mL) of the broth into **(1-cup/250-mL) Prep Bowl**; microwave on HIGH 30-60 seconds or until boiling. Carefully remove from microwave. Add mushrooms; let stand 10 minutes. Remove mushrooms from broth and thinly slice; set aside in broth.

2 As mushrooms soak, slice green onions; set green tops aside for garnish. Lightly spray **(4-qt./3.8-L) Casserole** with oil using **Kitchen Spritzer**. Heat over medium-high heat 1-3 minutes or until hot. Add remaining onions; cook and stir 1 minute or until tender. Add remaining broth, vinegar, soy sauce, curry paste and mushroom mixture. Cover and bring to a boil.

3 Meanwhile, peel carrots; cut into short julienne strips using **Julienne Peeler**. Add carrots to soup; reduce to a simmer and cook 5 minutes.

4 Whisk together cornstarch and water in same Prep Bowl. Whisk into soup; simmer 5 minutes. Meanwhile, drain tofu and cut into ½-in. (1-cm) cubes; add to soup.

5 Remove Casserole from heat. Lightly beat eggs in **Small Batter Bowl**; drizzle into soup. Cover and let stand 5 minutes or until eggs are cooked. Garnish with reserved onion tops and serve.

U.S. Nutrients per serving (1½ cups/375 mL): Calories 140, Total Fat 6 g, Saturated Fat 1 g, Cholesterol 105 mg, Carbohydrate 13 g, Protein 10 g, Sodium 990 mg, Fiber 2 g

U.S. Diabetic exchanges per serving: ½ starch, 1 vegetable, 1 medium-fat meat (½ carb)

COOK'S TIPS

Tofu has a bland flavor that enables it to take on the flavor of the food it is served with. Tofu is available in a variety of textures ranging from firm to silken, which is smooth and creamy. It is low in calories and high in protein.

Shiitake mushrooms have a full-bodied, woodsy flavor. They are available dried and fresh. Fresh can be substituted without soaking.

Thai red curry paste is a spicy blend of spices and chiles. It is available in the Asian section of most grocery stores.

quick and creamy mac 'n cheese

A SURPRISING INGREDIENT HELPS CREATE A HEALTHIER VERSION OF A FAMILY FAVORITE.

Total Time: 19 minutes   **Yield:** 6 servings

16 oz (450 g) uncooked medium shell pasta

1 pkg (12 oz/350 g) frozen butternut squash, thawed

1 can (12 oz or 370 mL) evaporated milk

2 cups (500 mL) shredded six-cheese Italian cheese blend

½ tsp (2 mL) salt

⅛ tsp (0.5 mL) ground nutmeg

Additional ground nutmeg (optional)

1 For pasta, bring salted water to a boil in covered **(4-qt./3.8-L) Casserole**. Cook pasta according to package directions. Carefully remove ¼ cup (50 mL) of the cooking water for later use. Drain pasta; return to Casserole and set aside.

2 For sauce, place squash into **(3-qt./2.8-L) Saucepan**; gradually add milk, whisking constantly using **Silicone Sauce Whisk**. Cook over medium-high heat 3-4 minutes or until mixture begins to simmer. Reduce heat to medium. Add cheese; cook 3-4 minutes or until cheese is melted and mixture returns to a simmer, whisking constantly. Add salt, nutmeg and reserved cooking water; stir until smooth. Add sauce to pasta; mix to coat.

3 To serve, divide pasta among serving bowls; sprinkle with additional ground nutmeg, if desired.

U.S. Nutrients per serving: Calories 500, Total Fat 14 g, Saturated Fat 8 g, Cholesterol 45 mg, Carbohydrate 68 g, Protein 24 g, Sodium 520 mg, Fiber 3 g

U.S. Diabetic exchanges per serving: 4½ starch, 2 medium-fat meat (4½ carb)

COOK'S TIPS

Butternut squash adds creaminess and a pleasant yellow-orange color, which makes a great substitution for some of the cheese in this classic dish. Whisking the evaporated milk with the squash breaks down the squash and blends it into the mixture.

Evaporated milk contributes richness and creaminess without adding a lot of fat.

Italian cheese blends require smaller quantities to lend assertive cheese taste. Any Italian cheese blend can be used in this recipe.

Using some of the pasta cooking water has a dual purpose: the starch in the water helps to thicken the sauce, and since it's warm, the overall cook time is slightly reduced even further when preparing this recipe.

harvest cream soup

THIS UPSCALE PUREED SOUP, FINISHED WITH A SPLASH OF FRESH GINGER
JUICE AND A SWIRL OF SOUR CREAM, IS REMARKABLY EASY TO MAKE.

Total Time: 60 minutes **Yield:** 6 servings

1 lb (450 g) butternut squash

2 leeks (white and light green portions only)

1 lb (450 g) baby carrots (about 3 cups/750 mL)

1 tbsp (15 mL) olive oil

1 garlic clove, pressed

   Salt and coarsely ground black pepper (optional)

2 cans (14.5 oz each) vegetable broth (about
   4 cups/1 L), divided

1 can (12 oz or 370 mL) evaporated milk

1 1-in (2.5-cm) piece unpeeled fresh gingerroot

   Reduced-fat sour cream (optional)

1 Preheat oven to 450°F (230°C). Cut squash into 1-in. (2.5-cm) pieces. Cut leeks in half lengthwise (see Cook's Tip), then into 2-in. (5-cm) pieces. Combine squash, leeks, carrots, oil and garlic pressed with **Garlic Press** in **Stainless (6-qt./6-L) Mixing Bowl**; toss to coat using **Mix 'N Scraper®**. Season with salt and black pepper, if desired.

2 Arrange vegetables in a single layer on **Large Bar Pan**. Bake 40-45 minutes or until vegetables are tender and deep golden brown. Remove pan from oven to **Stackable Cooling Rack**.

3 Combine half of the vegetables with half of the broth in blender container. Cover; blend until smooth. Pour vegetable puree into **(4-qt./3.8-L) Casserole**. Repeat with remaining vegetable mixture and broth. Add evaporated milk to Casserole; mix well. Cook over medium heat 5-6 minutes or until heated through, stirring occasionally.

4 Grate gingerroot using **Microplane® Adjustable Grater**. Gather gingerroot in palm of hand and squeeze over **(1-cup/250-mL) Prep Bowl** to yield 2 tsp (10 mL); discard flesh. Stir juice into soup just before serving. Season to taste with salt and black pepper. Ladle soup into bowls; swirl in sour cream, if desired.

U.S. Nutrients per serving: Calories 180, Total Fat 7 g, Saturated Fat 3 g, Cholesterol 20 mg, Carbohydrate 24 g, Protein 6 g, Sodium 900 mg, Fiber 5 g

U.S. Diabetic exchanges per serving: 1 starch, 2 vegetable, 1 fat (1 carb)

COOK'S TIPS

To clean leeks, cut in half lengthwise and rinse thoroughly to remove all of the sand and grit.

The white and light green parts of leeks are the most tender portions. Do not use the dark green leaves.

pan-fried polenta with vegetable marinara

KEEP TUBES OF PREPARED POLENTA ON HAND FOR THIS HEARTY MEAL.

Total Time: 25 minutes   **Yield:** 2 servings

Coating and Polenta

2 tbsp (30 mL) all-purpose flour

1/8 tsp (0.5 mL) coarsely ground black pepper

1 egg

1 oz (30 g) Parmesan cheese, grated (about 1/4 cup/50 mL)

1/4 cup (50 mL) dry bread crumbs

1 1-lb (450-g) tube prepared polenta

2 tbsp (30 mL) olive oil

2 tbsp (30 mL) butter

Additional grated Parmesan cheese (optional)

Vegetable Marinara

1 tbsp (15 mL) olive oil

1 medium zucchini

8 oz (250 g) sliced mushrooms

1 cup (250 mL) marinara sauce

1 For coating, combine flour and black pepper in **Coating Tray**. Lightly beat egg in second tray. Grate cheese using **Rotary Grater**. Combine cheese with bread crumbs in third tray.

2 To coat polenta, slice ends off polenta; discard ends. Slice into eight 3/4-inch-thick (2-cm) rounds. Lightly dredge rounds in flour mixture, shaking off excess; dip into egg and then into bread crumb mixture. Set aside.

3 For marinara, add oil to **(3-qt./2.8-L) Saucepan**; heat over medium-high heat 1-3 minutes or until shimmering. Dice zucchini using **Santoku Knife**. Add zucchini and mushrooms to Saucepan. Cook 3-5 minutes or until vegetables are tender. Stir in marinara sauce; simmer 5 minutes.

4 Meanwhile, to finish polenta, place oil and butter into **(10-in./24-cm) Skillet**; heat over medium heat 1-3 minutes or until butter is foamy. Add polenta rounds to Skillet. Cook 1-2 minutes on each side or until golden brown. Remove from Skillet using **Small Slotted Turner**.

5 To serve, spoon marinara over polenta and top with additional grated Parmesan cheese, if desired.

U.S. Nutrients per serving: Calories 630, Total Fat 26 g, Saturated Fat 9 g, Cholesterol 130 mg, Carbohydrate 78 g, Protein 21 g, Sodium 1410 mg, Fiber 7 g

U.S. Diabetic exchanges per serving: 5 starch, 1 medium-fat meat, 3 fat (5 carb)

COOK'S TIPS

Pre-cooked polenta, available in the ethnic section of most grocery stores in sausage-shaped tubes, saves time required for cooking and cooling. Polenta doesn't need refrigeration before opening, so it is nice to have on hand for quick and easy last-minute meals.

Polenta is a staple in northern Italy and is often served as a soft, creamy porridge made with coarsely ground cornmeal. It can also be made using less water (as seen in this recipe) and sliced.

mediterranean hummus pizza

HUMMUS AND FLAVORFUL VEGETABLES TOP A THIN
PIZZA CRUST FOR A SATISFYING MEATLESS MAIN DISH.

Total Time: 20 minutes **Yield:** 6 servings

Crust

- 1 tbsp (15 mL) plus ½ tsp (2 mL) olive oil, divided
- 1 pkg (13.8 oz or 283 g) refrigerated pizza crust
- 1 garlic clove, pressed

Toppings

- 2 jars (7.5 oz or 170 mL each) quartered marinated artichoke hearts, drained
- 2 medium plum tomatoes
- ¼ medium red onion
- 1 2-in. (5-cm) piece seedless cucumber
- ½ cup (125 mL) pitted kalamata olives
- 1 container (7 oz or 283 g) plain hummus
- 2 oz (60 g) Mediterranean-seasoned feta cheese crumbles (⅓ cup/75 mL)

1 Preheat oven to 425°F (220°C). Lightly brush **Large Bar Pan** with ½ tsp (2 mL) of the oil using **Chef's Silicone Basting Brush**. Unroll dough onto bottom of pan, gently stretching and pressing dough to cover bottom. Combine remaining oil and garlic pressed with **Garlic Press** in **(1-cup/250-mL) Prep Bowl**; brush evenly over dough. Bake 12-14 minutes or until crust is light golden brown.

2 Meanwhile, for toppings, cut artichokes crosswise into smaller pieces using **Utility Knife**. Slice tomatoes in half lengthwise; scrape out seeds and dice. Thinly slice onion. Using **Ultimate Mandoline** fitted with v-shaped blade, slice cucumber; cut slices into quarters. Coarsely chop olives using **Food Chopper**.

3 Remove pan from oven to **Stackable Cooling Rack**. Spread hummus evenly over crust. Arrange artichokes, tomatoes, onion, cucumber and olives over hummus. Sprinkle with cheese. Cut pizza into squares using **Pizza Cutter**.

U.S. Nutrients per serving: Calories 310, Total Fat 13 g, Saturated Fat 2 g, Cholesterol 0 mg, Carbohydrate 42 g, Protein 10 g, Sodium 950 mg, Fiber 4 g

U.S. Diabetic exchanges per serving: 2½ starch, 1 vegetable, 2 fat (2½ carb)

COOK'S TIPS

Any flavored hummus can be substituted for the plain hummus, if desired.

To easily remove seeds from tomatoes, cut tomatoes in half lengthwise and use the **Core & More** to scrape out the seeds.

sweet potato tagine with pine nut couscous

THIS AROMATIC, MOROCCAN-INSPIRED DISH IS SURE TO BE A DINNERTIME FAVORITE.

Total Time: 22 minutes   **Yield:** 4 servings

- 8 oz (250 g) sweet potatoes, peeled
- 1 small onion
- 2 garlic cloves, peeled
- 1 tbsp (15 mL) olive oil
- 2 tbsp (30 mL) **Moroccan Rub**
- 2 medium plum tomatoes
- ¾ cup (175 mL) loosely packed fresh cilantro
- 1 can (15 oz/540 mL) chickpeas, drained and rinsed
- 2½ cups (625 mL) vegetable broth
- 1 pkg (5.6 oz or 160 g) toasted pine nut-flavored couscous

1. Cut sweet potatoes in half horizontally then vertically using **Santoku Knife**. Slice sweet potatoes and onion using **Ultimate Mandoline** fitted with v-shaped blade. Slice garlic with **Garlic Slicer**; set aside

2. Heat oil in **(10-in./24-cm) Skillet** over medium heat 1-3 minutes or until shimmering. Add sweet potatoes, onion and rub; cook 5-6 minutes or until onion is tender, stirring occasionally.

3. Meanwhile, seed and dice tomatoes. Chop cilantro using **Chef's Knife**; set aside. Add tomatoes, chickpeas, broth, garlic and seasoning packet from couscous to Skillet; mix well and bring to a boil. Stir in couscous; cover and remove from heat. Let stand 5 minutes. Garnish with cilantro.

U.S. Nutrients per serving: Calories 290, Total Fat 6 g, Saturated Fat 1 g, Cholesterol 0 mg, Carbohydrate 51 g, Protein 10 g, Sodium 1140 mg, Fiber 7 g

U.S. Diabetic exchanges per serving: 3 starch, 1 vegetable, ½ fat (3 carb)

COOK'S TIPS

Thinly slicing rather than pressing the garlic gives the dish a slightly mellower garlic flavor.

A tagine (tuh-JEEN) is a traditional Moroccan stew that is slow-cooked over low heat and typically served over couscous.

Chickpeas are often found in Moroccan cooking and provide protein for a satisfying main dish.

roasted vegetable & sizzling brown rice soup

ROASTED VEGETABLES ADD A SLIGHTLY SMOKY, CARAMELIZED FLAVOR
TO DISHES, BUT TIME IS OFTEN AN ISSUE. ROASTING VEGETABLES
QUICKLY IS POSSIBLE WITH THE RIGHT TECHNIQUE.

Total Time: 22 minutes **Yield:** 8 servings

6 cups (1.5 L) vegetable broth

2 cans (14.5 oz or 398 mL each) diced tomatoes
  with green chiles, undrained

1 medium zucchini

1 medium yellow squash

8 oz (250 g) asparagus spears, trimmed

2 garlic cloves, pressed

2 tbsp (30 mL) vegetable oil, divided

2 pouches (8.8 oz/250 g each) cooked brown rice

1 Preheat broiler. Bring broth and tomatoes to a boil in covered **(4-qt./3.8-L)
Casserole**. Meanwhile, dice zucchini and squash into ½-in. (1-cm) pieces.
Cut asparagus into 1-in. (2.5-cm) pieces. Toss vegetables, pressed garlic
and 1 tbsp (15 mL) of the oil in **Stainless (6-qt./6-L) Mixing Bowl**. Arrange
vegetables in a single layer over **Large Sheet Pan**. Place pan 2-4 in. (5-10 cm)
from heating element. Broil 4-5 minutes or until crisp-tender.

2 Heat remaining 1 tbsp (15 mL) oil in **(10-in./24-cm) Skillet** over medium-high
heat 1-3 minutes or until shimmering. Separate rice according to package
directions. Evenly distribute rice over bottom of Skillet; cover with **Splatter
Screen**. Cook without stirring 5-6 minutes or until rice is golden and crisp.
Remove Skillet from heat; let stand, covered with screen, 1 minute. Remove
Casserole from heat; add roasted vegetables. To serve, ladle soup into serving
bowls; top with rice.

U.S. Nutrients per serving (2 cups/500 mL): Calories 180, Total Fat 5 g, Saturated Fat 0 g,
Cholesterol 0 mg, Carbohydrate 28 g, Protein 4 g, Sodium 1130 mg, Fiber 3 g

U.S. Diabetic exchanges per serving: 1 starch, 2 vegetable, 1 fat (1 carb)

COOK'S TIPS

Toasting the layer of rice on one side gives a range of textures to one ingredient with minimal preparation. The Splatter Screen is helpful
to contain the stray pieces of rice that can otherwise pop right out of the Skillet.

If desired, 4 cups (1 L) cold cooked brown rice can be substituted for the rice pouches.

When roasting vegetables, it's important to cut them uniformly so they will cook evenly.

This is a recipe than can be made with a variety of vegetables such as bell peppers, onions or eggplant.